Buzz, Bee!

Jennifer Szymanski

NATIONAL GEOGRAPHIC

Washington, D.C.

Vocabulary Tree

ANIMALS

HONEYBEES

WHAT THEY NEED TO LIVE

nectar
pollen
hive
honey

WHAT THEY DO

buzz
fly
eat
drink
dance

Buzz, bee!

A bee flies in the air.

It looks for a flower.

There's a sweet treat in flowers.
It's called nectar.

The bee drinks.

The bee eats.
It eats pollen.

Bees carry pollen in a basket on their legs.

It gets pollen to take home.

A bee's home is called a hive.

Many bees live in the hive.

Bees put pollen in the hive.

Once nectar becomes honey, bees put it in a honeycomb.

They make honey
from nectar, too.

Now there's food in the hive.

Other bees can eat the
pollen and honey.

In the hive, a bee dances.

The dance tells other bees where to find nectar.

The bee moves from side to side. This is called a "waggle dance."

18 The bees fly out of the hive.

They look for the nectar.

They use the dance to find
the right flower!

Buzz, bee!

NECTAR AND POLLEN:
What are they like?

Nectar drips.
It's sweet.

Pollen is made up
of tiny balls.
It's like powder.

YOUR TURN!

Think of a spot in the room. Do a "waggle" dance to tell your friend how to get there! Then switch roles.

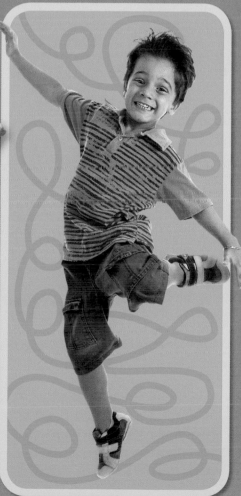

AUTHOR'S NOTE: There are many different kinds of bees. In this book, the word "bee" refers specifically to honeybees.

The publisher gratefully acknowledges the expert content review of this book by Dr. William O. Lamp, University of Maryland, Department of Entomology, and the expert literacy review of this book by Kimberly Gillow, Principal, Milan Area Schools, Michigan.

Designed by Sanjida Rashid

Library of Congress Cataloging-in-Publication Data

Names: Szymanski, Jennifer, author.
Title: National Geographic readers. Buzz, bee! / Jennifer Szymanski.
Other titles: Buzz, bee!
Description: Washington, DC : National Geographic, 2017. | Series: National Geographic readers | Audience: Ages 2 to 5. | Audience: Pre-school.
Identifiers: LCCN 2016041805 (print) | LCCN 2016055235 (ebook) | ISBN 9781426327803 (pbk. : alk. paper) | ISBN 9781426327810 (hardcover: alk. paper) | ISBN 9781426327827 () | ISBN 9781426327834
Subjects: LCSH: Bees--Juvenile literature.
Classification: LCC QL565.2 .S99 2017 (print) | LCC QL565.2 (ebook) | DDC 595.79/9--dc23
LC record available at https://lccn.loc.gov/2016041805

Photo Credits
Cover, Antagain/Getty Images; 1 (CTR), Joerg Hauke/Getty Images; 2–3 (CTR), Michael Durham/Minden Pictures; 4–5 (CTR), Phil Savoie/Minden Pictures; 6–7 (CTR), Musat/Getty Images; 8 (CTR), Konrad Wothe/Minden Pictures; 9 (CTR), kojihirano/Getty Images; 10–11 (CTR), Emily Skeels/Shutterstock; 12 (CTR), Stephen Dalton/Minden Pictures; 13 (CTR), greenantphoto/Getty Images; 14–15 (CTR), temmuzcan/Getty Images; 16–17 (CTR), Paul Starosta/Getty Images; 18–19 (CTR), photofxs68/Getty Images; 20 (CTR), Sumiko Scott/Getty Images; 21 (CTR), Michael Durham/Minden Pictures; 22 (UP), Heidi and Hans-Juergen Koch/Minden Pictures; 22 (LO), Konrad Wothe/Minden Pictures; 23 (LE), KidStock/Getty Images; 23 (RT), MarcusVDT/Shutterstock; 24 (UP), Phil Savoie/Nature Picture Library

Printed in the United States of America
17/WOR/2